ULSTER ARCHITECTURAL HERITAGE SOCIETY
SURVEY AND RECOMMENDATIONS
FOR THE
JOY STREET & HAMILTON STREET
DISTRICT OF
BELFAST

prepared   July 1970 - March 1971

by

C.E.B. Brett
R. McKinstry
for the
Ulster Architectural Heritage Society

This Survey is the outcome of a meeting between members of the Society and the Town Planning Committee on 2nd June 1970. The compilers gratefully acknowledge much helpful information made available to them by residents or former residents in the area, and particularly by Mr. Joe Sherrie. The engraving of St. Malachy's church on the front cover, from James O'Hagan's map of 1848, is reproduced by permission of the Trustees of the Ulster Museum. The maps on page 3 are reproduced by courtesy of the Governors of the Linenhall Library, and the Public Record Office of Northern Ireland. The photograph of St. Malachy's on page 14 is by Mr. Sean Watters; that of University Street on the same page by Mr. Robert McKinstry; all the other photographs were specially taken by Mr. Neil Marshall.

The area bounded by May Street, Alfred Street, Ormeau Avenue, and Cromac Street - sometimes known as the 'Upper Markets' to distinguish it from the 'Low Markets' district on the other side of Cromac Street - is a mixed residential and commercial area with a very definite identity of its own. It lies close to the commercial centre of Belfast, and close also to the early 20th century linen warehousing district centred on Bedford Street. But, apart from a crust of office, commercial, shopping, and small industrial premises around the edges, it is a compact community of private residents, almost indeed a village within the city, whose heart is St. Malachy's church.

Historically, this was one of the most interesting extensions of the 18th century town of Belfast. It came after the first effects of the industrial revolution, but before the vast influx of workers which accompanied the Great Famine. The district spread gradually southwards from May Street. Originally the wide and marshy tidal waters of the Lagan came up to a causeway ("the Bank") running more or less from Cornmarket to the site of the Power Station in Laganbank Road; the water-powered 18th century paper mill of the Joy family stood near Ormeau Avenue; the Blackstaff river entered the Lagan, as it does now, through an artificial cut (created early in the 18th century by the third Lord Donegall as an unemployment relief scheme); and the greater part of the upper markets is built on land reclaimed from the wide and shallow mill-pond. A reflection of this may be found in the fact that the houses north of Hamilton Street suffer considerably less from rising damp than those to the south of it: and indeed, this substratum will need to be taken into account by the architects of any future redevelopment. George Benn, in 1823, wrote of the area - "There was formerly an extensive wood, principally consisting of oaks, reaching from May's Market... to the Lagan, and along the bank of that river to the present New Bridge" (the old Ormeau Bridge). "Many of the old inhabitants recollect this wood, which was principally remarkable for the great number of swans which built their nests in it." The oaks, alas, have all gone, but the swans stubbornly survive.

The upper markets were built a little earlier than the low markets, and for a rather more prosperous class of residents - though there are some fine houses in the low markets too, especially in New Bond Street. The large terraces at the northern end of Alfred Street and Joy Street, and in Sussex Place and Hamilton Street, were the homes of highly respectable merchants, little less grand than the slightly earlier houses in Chichester Street, Wellington Place, and Donegall Square and Place. The flight of the middle classes to the suburbs - especially the Malone ridge - only really started in the 1840s and 1850s. The Duke of Abercorn's town house (demolished only in 1962) was at No. 3 Hamilton Street, and the street bears his family name. May Street and Joy Street perpetuate the names of well-known Belfast families; Sussex Place, Adelaide Street, and Clarence Place were all named after members of the royal family before the accession of Queen Victoria. It does not seem to be remembered who Grace, Catherine and Henrietta were.

As the century moved on, the wealthier classes tended more and more to move to the new suburbs built on higher ground. The large houses they vacated in this district were extremely well suited for use as respectable boarding-houses; and after the foundation of the Queen's College in 1849, this became a favourite district for students to lodge. Gradually the students tended to move closer to the college as the University Road and Ormeau Road areas developed in the 1850s, 1860s and 1870s. But a strong sense of identification with the University survived well into this century; the residents used to attend all the students' sports meetings. They used also to attend cycling races and to cheer on John Boyd Dunlop's riders on their newly invented pneumatic tyres - for the whole development of the Dunlop tyre took place in these streets, since Dunlop, a veterinary surgeon, had premises in Gloucester Street and in May Street, and was a well-known and popular figure.

As the students moved out of the area, their places were taken by business lodgers, and above all by musical and theatrical personalities. The older residents in Joy Street take great pride in their recollections of the days, before and immediately after the 1914 war, when all the well-known stars of the theatrical and entertainment world - from Charles Chaplin upwards and downwards -

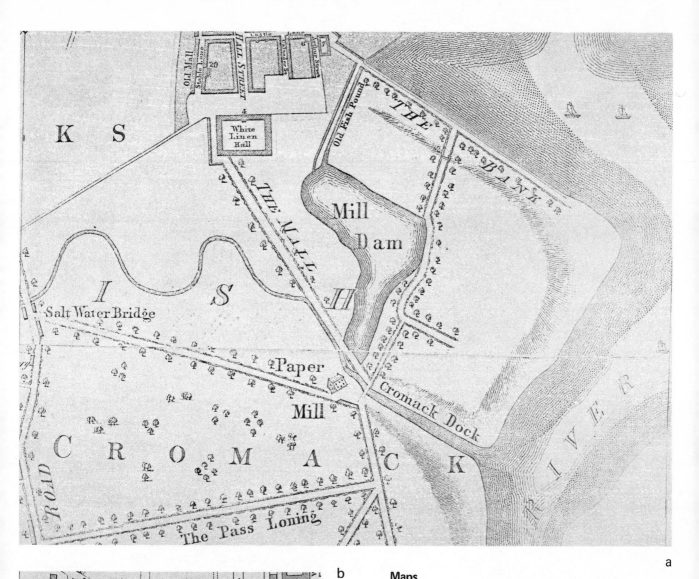

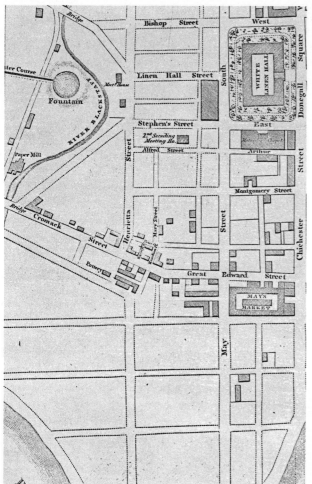

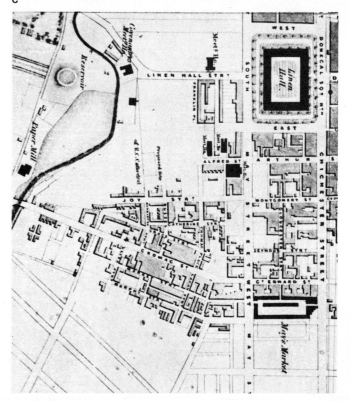

a

Maps

a From James Williamson's 'Map of the Town and Environs of Belfast', 1791

b From 'A new and correct plan of the Town of Belfast' by J. Thomson, 1823

c From map 'Drawn by James Kennedy, Surveyor, Bangor', 1838

b

c

used to stay here. This tradition lingered on until the closing of Belfast's last variety and repertory theatre, the Empire, a decade ago. Another tradition, not long extinct, relates to the entertainments - wrestling, boxing, and other - laid on by Mrs. Copley in the Chapel Fields (now built over, at the southern end of Alfred Street) especially during the years of depression between the wars.

The feeling of community within the district is exceptionally strong. Many families have lived here for three or more generations: the girls have been educated together at the little convent school run by the Sisters of Mercy at the corner of Joy Street and Hamilton Street; the boys at the Oxford Street school of the Christian Brothers (closed very recently). Though this is now a mainly Catholic area, it was originally more mixed; relations have always been friendly and neighbourly. The older people have a great affection for the area, and for their homes, and have no wish to move. Younger people feel the lack of modern amenities more; most of them would prefer new houses with bathrooms as obviously more suitable for bringing up children; but many of them would like to stay in the district if this were possible. Apart from the ties of the family, community, school and church, there are considerable advantages in living so close to the centre of the town: those who work in city centre offices or shops have no fares to pay: and the shops and markets are within easy walking distance for the housewives. Many of the environmental amenities of life, however, are lacking; there is no convenient park or children's playground; there are only two mature trees in the whole area (both in the curtilege of St. Malachy's church); and the streets become ever more choked by moving traffic and by parked cars.

*   *   *   *   *

The foregoing historical and social notes do not deal with the architectural interest of the area. It contains one outstanding building - in the opinion of some authorities, the most important architecturally in Belfast - St. Malachy's church, built by Thomas Jackson in 1844; and this is the nucleus of the whole district. The May Street Presbyterian Church (1829, by W. Smith) is a particularly fine example of the late Georgian classical tradition. The residential terraces of the 1820s and 1830s, though in no instance particularly distinguished, constitute much the best example left in the city of late-Georgian Belfast: it is to be remembered that there is a provincial time-lag - the Georgian tradition lingered longer in Ireland than in England, and longer in the north than in Dublin; indeed it cannot be said to have died in Belfast until the 1870's.

The district is described in the following terms in "Buildings of Belfast, 1700-1914" by C.E.B. Brett (London, Weidenfeld & Nicholson, 1967) at page 20:

"The leisurely development of the Georgian terrace house can be studied instructively in the area around Joy Street, Hamilton Street, and the district known as 'the Markets', most of which was built in the 1830s and '40s on land reclaimed either from the tide or from the former dam of the Cromac paper-mill. There are plain brick terraces of great character at 2-32 Joy Street and 4-18 Sussex Place; again at 7-19, 35-41 and 36-46 Hamilton Street (7 has an odd but pleasing massive Norman-Regency pointed doorway); and a fine stucco terrace at 20-30 Hamilton Street, set back a few feet from the street line, with hooded doorways, light pilasters, an ornamental frieze, acroteria, and a rusticated ground floor. This district more than any other gives a vivid impression of Belfast as it was before the full gale-force of Victorian industrial expansion struck. Most of the houses are in fair order, respectable, and cared-for by their tenants, if not always by their landlords. It would be well worth preserving at least a selection of them when the time for redevelopment comes."

Several of the buildings in the district are referred to, or illustrated, in "The Changing Face of Belfast", a booklet by Mr. Noel Nesbitt, published by the Ulster Museum in 1968.

a

b

c

d

e

f

g

h

Doorcases, Fanlights and Boot-Scrapers

a   61, Joy Street
b   30, Hamilton Street
c   14, Alfred Street
d   4, Alfred Street
e   69, Joy Street
f   79, Joy Street
g   38, Hamilton Street
h   26, Joy Street
i   40 and 42, Hamilton Street
j   78, Joy Street
k   40, Little May Street
l   4, Joy Street
m   20, Hamilton Street

i

j

k

l

m

A large number of the buildings within the district are singled out for mention in the 'Building Preservation Policy' report prepared by Building Design Partnership as part of the Belfast Development Plan and published in August 1966. This document should be referred to for the more extensive descriptions it contains. Those listed include May Street Presbyterian Church; Nos. 14-26 Joy Street; Nos. 28-32 Joy Street; Nos. 20-30 Hamilton Street; Nos. 42-52, 54-90, 45-55, and 57-107 Joy Street; St. Malachy's Church; and McWatters Bakery at 92-102 Joy Street.

The sub-committee of the Ancient Monuments Advisory Council appointed in March 1966 to advise on buildings of importance in Belfast, which included co-opted representatives of Belfast Corporation, recommended as follows:

"Private dwellings, Hamilton Street - Joy Street; Best houses are 14-26 Joy Street. Period 1845. B. Measured drawings should be prepared at once of this fine terrace in an area to be redeveloped, and the block scheduled. A good case could be made for retaining these houses as an excellent illustration of Georgian housing in pre-industrial Belfast."

On 2nd June 1970 Mr. C.E.B. Brett and Mr. R. McKinstry, on behalf of the U.A.H.S., appeared before the town planning Committee; and at its meeting on 15th June 1970 Mr. Booth, the City Planning Officer, tabled a report which included the following paragraph:

"6. Following the interest expressed by several committee members in a proposal for the preservation and modernisation of a number of terrace houses in the Hamilton Street/Joy Street area, it was confirmed that the Society would be happy to undertake the preparation of a paper outlining its proposals which would then be submitted to the Planning Officer."

This paper represents the preliminary outcome of that undertaking. It does not, at this stage, advance proposals; but it may constitute a useful basis on which proposals, taking into account other factors in the redevelopment, can be formulated.

         *   *   *   *   *

The detailed notes on buildings within the district which follow take account of architectural, visual, and historical considerations, but no examination has been made of the structural state of the buildings. Many of them are clearly in poor condition, but modern techniques of restoration can now overcome most difficulties, including the absence of damp-courses.

The method of classification in this instance departs from that employed in the Society's other Lists of Buildings. Those considered of particular merit or importance are marked A; those considered important because of their visual or environmental contribution to a group or vista of buildings are marked A/B; those which are of less interest, but might be incorporated in a scheme for a larger group or axis, are marked B; those which substantially detract from the environment, and which should ideally be demolished and replaced by environmentally more satisfactory development, are marked X. It is appreciated that so drastic a course would only be feasible on wholesale redevelopment of the area.

RECOMMENDATIONS

1.   There are two possible methods of approaching a renewal scheme in the area.
      The first, which is the more ambitious but would probably prove the more satisfactory, is the 'axis' approach. This would involve the retention and restoration of most of the buildings in the A, A/B and B categories on both sides of Joy Street, and on both sides of Hamilton Street. In a number of cases, almost complete reconstruction would be required behind the facades; but this approach would have the advantage of retaining the character of the district, and of allowing individual buildings to be seen three-dimensionally in the context of their historical environment.

The second - the 'spot' approach - involves the retention of the street pattern within a smaller area and keeping only the buildings which are both of outstanding merit and in reasonable order, accompanied by an endeavour to provide new buildings beside and between them which are harmonious in scale, proportions, detailing, and materials. This might well be more economical, but it might well prove an extremely difficult exercise. Modern brickwork, roofing, door and window details, all differ substantially in character from those to be found in the district; the historical feeling and individuality of the area would be lost, and such individual houses or groups as were retained might stand out singly like museum exhibits. To build "Georgian reproduction" dwellings on the sites of those demolished would be neither historically nor architecturally sound.

The notes and map which follow are designed to make possible an assessment of the 'axis' approach: the importance attaching to groups (as against individual buildings) is now widely recognised (compare the Civic Amenities Act, 1967, in Great Britain), and this course is considered strongly preferable. But if the 'spot' approach must be selected, it is hoped that the list will nonetheless be of value; in that case, it is urged that the crossing of Joy Street and Hamilton Street be treated as the nucleus of any conservation scheme, and that Nos. 4-32 and 9-39 Joy Street, Nos. 20-46 and 39-41 Hamilton Street, and Nos. 2 and 4 Sussex Place, be retained, so that a genuinely three-dimensional example of late Georgian Belfast may be preserved.

2.   A feasibility study should be undertaken by the City Planning Department. The compilers of this Preliminary Survey, and the Committee of the U.A.H.S., will be happy to give all possible help and assistance; but good replanning is a matter for professionals, not amateurs, and must take account of such matters as future traffic patterns, educational needs, and so on.

If the assumption is made that the Markets area is to be redeveloped for mainly residential purposes, it is suggested that many of the buildings listed could well be integrated into new developments, either as restored residences for the older people, or to meet other social needs. In particular, it is recommended that the gaps between terraces of architectural importance might be used partly for open space and recreational purposes, but principally for small shops, services, and craftsmen, such as might constitute a socially useful middle-ground between a commercial and a residential area. It will have been noticed that art galleries and antique shops have shown a recent tendency to gravitate towards May Street; this spontaneous tendency might well be encouraged; some of the specialist concerns in and around Smithfield market might be rehoused here, as well as watch and clock repairers, shoe repairers, the blacksmith from Eliza Street, picture framers, and other small specialist concerns.

3.   Pending the completion of this study, no further demolitions within the area should be permitted. It is a sad fact that property owners are now finding vacant space for car-parking more remunerative than controlled housing. The destruction in 1970 of the excellent terrace at 4-18 Sussex Place has greatly detracted from the coherence of the whole area. The conversion of 3 Hamilton Street (the Duke of Abercorn's town house) to commercial use was a severe loss.

4.   Existing planning legislation does notpermit the Corporation to veto demolitions, except in the case of listed Ancient Monuments; it is unlikely that any of the buildings (other than churches) in this preliminary survey would qualify for listing under the present legislation.

But there is a simple, and socially useful, solution: the Corporation should exercise its powers of compulsory acquisition whenever one of the buildings listed is vacant, or freed from control under the Rent Restriction Acts or Business Tenancies Acts.

Already, a fair number of dwelling-houses within the district are vacant, in some cases with their windows bricked up. While these are technically 'unfit' buildings they could very usefully be employed during the present acute housing crisis to provide temporary accomodation, with only minimal expenditure. Examples of fine houses at present empty and wasted are to be seen at No. 14 Joy Street; Nos. 30 and 32 Joy Street; and No. 30 Hamilton Street. It is very strongly recommended that the Corporation should at once acquire these, and put them in sufficiently good order to allow them to be tenanted pending decisions on long-term development.

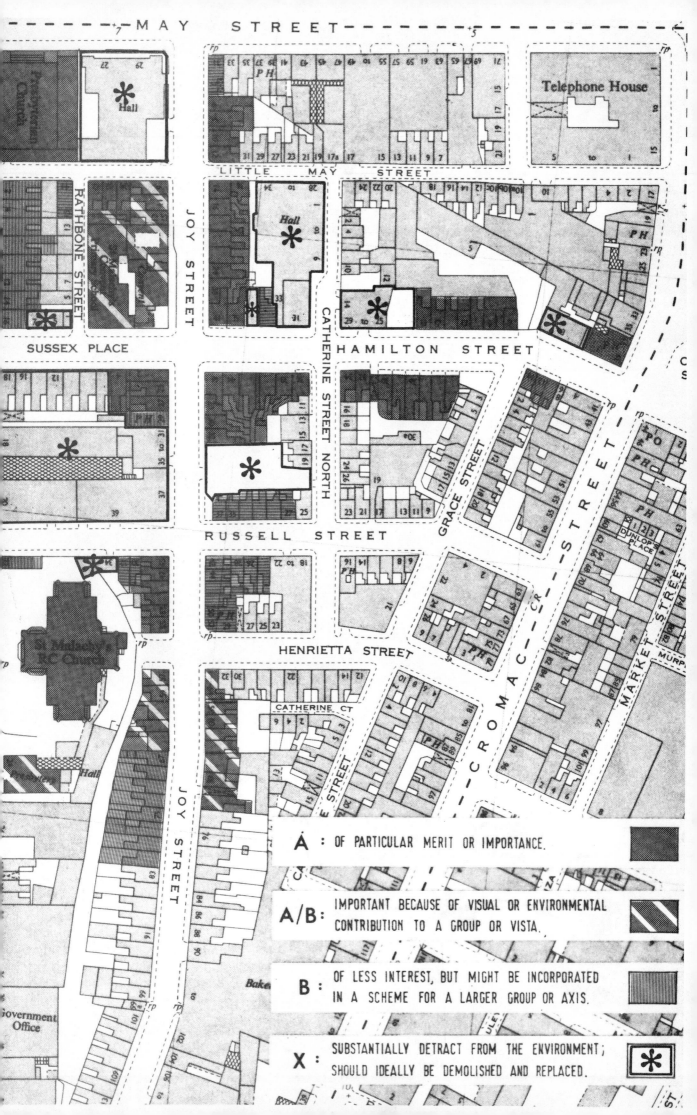

MAY STREET

Presbyterian Church

Hall

Telephone House

LITTLE MAY STREET

RATHBONE STREET

JOY STREET

Hall

CATHERINE STREET NORTH

PH

SUSSEX PLACE

HAMILTON STREET

GRACE STREET

STREET

PO
PH

PH
DUNLOP'S
PLACE

RUSSELL STREET

St. Malachy's
RC Church

CATHERINE CT

HENRIETTA STREET

PH

PH

CROMAC CR.

MARKET STREET

MURPH

Hall

PH

JOY STREET

Baker

Government
Office

A : OF PARTICULAR MERIT OR IMPORTANCE.

A/B : IMPORTANT BECAUSE OF VISUAL OR ENVIRONMENTAL
CONTRIBUTION TO A GROUP OR VISTA.

B : OF LESS INTEREST, BUT MIGHT BE INCORPORATED
IN A SCHEME FOR A LARGER GROUP OR AXIS.

X : SUBSTANTIALLY DETRACT FROM THE ENVIRONMENT;
SHOULD IDEALLY BE DEMOLISHED AND REPLACED.

No.	Building	Class	Date, Type, Architect, etc.	References
	ALFRED STREET: EAST SIDE			
1.	May St./Alfred St.	A	Presbyterian Church, 1829, by W. Smith. See 'Buildings of Belfast', p. 17: "Architectural taste in Belfast at the end of the 1820s was becoming more sophisticated, more various, and more subject to outside influences. The next few years saw ventures not only in the Tudor, but also in the Greek Revival and the Palladian styles. One of the most satisfying of these is the May Street Presbyterian Church**, built in 1829 to the designs of W. Smith. Both inside and outside, it is a really handsome Palladian example of the Presbyterian taste for the solidly classical. There is a fine brick and stucco pedimented facade, with a recessed central entrance bay between 'Scamozzian Ionic' columns and pilasters arranged in antis. The contrasting patterns of painted stucco architraves and the ripe brickwork are beautifully judged, though the church would look better if the stucco were painted paler and oftener. Inside, there are twin curving staircases leading to a fine horseshoe gallery of polished mahogany, carried on cast-iron columns (also Scamozzian); excellent solid curving box-pews both on floor and gallery; and a good coffered timber ceiling, not over-ornamented though it dates only from 1872." See also the B.D.P. Report, Windsor Ward, no. 4; and the May Street Presbyterian Church Centenary Volume, by John Williamson, 1929. The adjoining stucco church hall is seemly and dignified.	Brett, p.17; Centenary Volume, 1929, passim; Changing Face of Belfast, pl 37; BDP Report, Windsor Ward, No. 4.
2.	Nos. 2-16 Alfred St.	B	A rather forbidding terrace of four-storey houses, rendered, with rudimentary pilasters; most glazing-bars complete; fine Ionic-pilaster doorcases at Nos. 2,4,6,8, and 10; good curly fanlights at Nos. 4 and 10; only No. 12 (Paddy Hopkirk) rather spoiled on conversion to a shop. If it were possible to hack off the rendering, and restore the Georgian brickwork, this terrace could look splendid; but this might be a slightly hazardous procedure. Alternatively, a scheme for suitable repainting of the stucco and shopfronts as a single unit could do wonders.	
3.	Block, Alfred Street, from Sussex Place to Russell Street.	X	No. 18 Sussex Place having been demolished, car-park and hoardings having been substituted, and the redbrick commercial premises at Nos. 18-20 Alfred Street being quite without visual merit, there seems nothing to be done here but to start again: perhaps with a garden opening up the end view of St. Malachy's?	
4.	St. Malachy's: gatelodge (No. 22, Alfred St.)	B	A redbrick cottage, mid-Victorian, with stone quoins, a quatrefoil window in the gable. Not worth preserving if a better scheme for the surroundings of St. Malachy's were adopted.	
5.	Beech tree behind the gatelodge.	A	Rarity value.	
6.	St. Malachy's Church	A	A splendid building by any standards. The site was acquired by Dr. Denvir in 1839, and was originally proposed as the site for a Roman Catholic cathedral for Belfast. An architectural competition was held; there were 14 entries; that of Thomas Jackson was chosen. His design clearly owes a good deal to the original design of his former partner, Thomas Duff of Newry, for Armagh Cathedral. The church was consecrated by the primate, Dr. Crolly, in 1844. The central tower seems to have been added later - it does not appear in the engraving of 1848. See O'Laverty, 'History of the Diocese of Down and Connor', Vol II, pp 424-427; and 'Buildings of Belfast', p. 23: "The finest late-Georgian building in Belfast is St. Malachy's Roman Catholic Church *** in Alfred Street, completed in 1844 by Thomas Jackson. It is a superb example of Sir-Walter-Scottery at its most romantic. The exterior, though of rather dingy brick, is	Brett, p 23, pls. 18 and 19; Centenary booklet, passim; O'Laverty, Vol II, pp 424-427; B.D.P. Report Windsor Ward, No. 12

No.	Building	Class	Date, Type, Architect, etc.	References
	St. Malachy's Church cont'd.		fine and dignified, soaring upwards in cruciform to lofty turrets and an oak tower (from which the spire was removed, with advantage; it is said because the tolling of the great bell in it interfered with the satisfactory maturing of the whiskey in Messrs. Dunville's adjacent distillery). The interior is enchanting: it is as though a wedding-cake had been turned inside-out, so creamy, lacy and frothy is the plasterwork. The ceiling is fan-vaulted in imitation of Henry VII's chapel in Westminster Abbey. The high altar is placed in one of the short arms of the cross to make more space - an extremely unusual departure from the traditional arrangement. Altar, reredos and pulpit are all pale and delightful. The altarpiece is by one of the Piccioni family, refugees to Belfast from Austrian Italy." See also B.D.P. Report, Windsor Ward, no 12.	
7.	St. Malachy's Presbytery, (No. 24, Alfred Street)	A/B	A three-storey four-square redbrick mid-Victorian house with hipped roof, coupled windows on ground floor, and polychrome black brick dressings. Part of the frame of the church; and insulates it from the early 20th century commercial buildings of the rest of Alfred Street southwards.	
	JOY STREET: WEST SIDE:			
8.	MaySt./Joy St.	X	The King George VI Memorial Hall. Too weak for the site; it neither provides a balancing note to the Presbyterian church, nor manages to turn the corner into May Street with confidence. As a contribution to the streetscape, two-dimensional.	
9.	Nos. 9-15 Joy Street	A/B	Plain three-storey brick houses without glazing bars; important principally as an echo of the better houses opposite. No. 9 (Connolly) has an unfortunate modern fascia; No. 11 has had its ground-floor rendered; Nos. 13/15 (Connolly again) incorporate a very nice shop-window of about 1850, above it one surviving wooden bracket-support with carved pears and pomegranates.	
10.	Convent of Mercy and School Joy St./Sussex Place.	A/B	1878, by Alex. McAlister, the leading Catholic church architect of his day. The Sisters of Mercy came to Belfast from Dublin in 1854; a branch convent was opened in 1858 at No. 15 Hamilton Street; the new school and convent were built with funds bequeathed by Mr. Bowen, proprietor of the Royal Hotel. Both are redbrick with stone detailing, the schools two-storey, the convent three-storey; inscribed "Young Ladies School"; a pleasant low tower with a campanile hat, an important landmark. If the school is to be removed elsewhere on redevelopment, and a modern building constructed, then it would scarcely be worth seeking a new function for this building; but if it is to remain, then it must be made a keystone of the new development. If the western parts of Sussex Place and Russell Street were closed, a garden-cum-school playground could be provided to link the convent directly to St. Malachy's. The area would be the poorer without its hordes of neatly-green-uniformed small girls.	O'Laverty, Vol II, pp 437-439; and the 'Irish Builder', 1879 p.274.
11.	Nos. 25 and 27, Joy Street	A	Excellent three-storey brick houses, with glazing bars complete, and geometrical fanlights.	
12.	The Grand Public House, No. 29, Joy Street	B	Stuccoed, with quoins, unsuitable new window-glazing and a horrible fascia; not beyond redemption as part of a group with its neighbours.	
13.	Nos. 31-37 Joy Street	X	Terrible red-brick commercial buildings.	

a

b

c

a   38-42, Little May Street
b   Convent of Mercy, Joy Street
c   4-12, Joy Street
d   May Street Presbyterian Church
e   19, Hamilton Street

e

d

No.	Building	Class	Date, Type, Architect, etc.	References
14.	Nos. 45-55 Joy Street	A	An outstandingly pleasant terrace of ordinary two-storey small houses of stucco, gaily painted, with excellent architraves and regency-style glazing bars. Behind 55 (at No. 55A) used to stand the Town Water Man's house, only recently turned into a garage.	
15.	Court at rear of St. Malachy's between 55 and 57 Joy Street.	A/B	An intriguing small open space, of which better use could be made; at present a park for mopeds.	
16.	Tree overhanging wall of Court.	A	Rarity value.	
17.	Nos. 57-65 Joy Street	A/B	Two-storey brick houses of some character, No. 61 with a particularly good fanlight and doorcase with reeded pilasters.	
18.	Nos. 67-81 Joy Street	B	Two-storey brick, Nos. 79 and 81 stuccoed; Nos. 69,71,73, 77, 79 and 81 retain Georgian astragal glazing-bars. Nos. 69,73, 79 and 81 have good fanlights.	
	JOY STREET: EAST SIDE:			
19.	May Street/Joy Street	B	A tall stucco gable that turns the corner with propriety.	
20.	Nos. 4-12 Joy Street	A	Fine three-storey stuccoed houses with stringcourse, quoins, architraves, and curving architraves to the doorcases. The cobbler's shop at No. 12 is a real amenity both to the neighbourhood and to the passing city gents who park here. The corner of the building is undercut, so that the shop entrance is at an angle to Joy Street and Little May Street - a rarish survivor of a once-common idiom.	'Changing Face of Belfast' pl 48
21.	Nos. 14-26 Joy Street.	A	A particularly fine terrace of tall three-storey redbrick houses with stone quoins, pilastered doorcases, and still some Georgian glazing-bars. Very well cared-for by the occupiers; two with bathrooms inserted by tenants. This and the preceding terrace are described in 'Changing Face of Belfast' as "good examples of late Georgian quality housing catering for the increasing number of well-to-do merchants and industrialists of the period... Houses of these types are often seen in Dublin but are all too rare in Belfast."	'Changing Face of Belfast' pl 48
22.	Nos. 28-32 Joy Street.	A	Another fine group, similar to Nos. 14-26, with medallions in the architraves above the fanlighted doorcases. No. 32, a fine house, lies shamefully empty, with broken windows.	
23.	Blitzed site, formerly Nos. 34-40 Joy Street	X	A yard, with an unsightly fence of corrugated iron.	
24.	Nos. 42-48 Joy Street	B	Redbrick houses, two-storey with attics, Georgian glazing-bars; No. 48 (Grocery and confectionery) has a very pleasant little traditional shop-window.	
25.	Joy Arms Pub, Nos. 50/52 Joy St.	B	A two-and-a half storey red brick pub of the early 20th century, with little pediments and scrolls at the dormers; homely rather than distinguished; the pub windows on the ground floor are framed in brick pilasters, the capitals incorporating a series of pleasantly grotesque faces, none readily recognisable.	

No.	Building	Class	Date, Type, Architect, etc.	References
26.	No. 54 Joy St.	A/B	A very old low house at the corner of Henrietta Street; two-storey brick with Georgian glazing bars and a tiny fanlight; held together by S-shaped tie-bars. Recently condemned, this is the oldest house in the district - a rural survival originally outside the confines of the town. Its historical importance should give it special consideration.	
27.	Nos. 58-66, Joy St.	A/B	Two-storeyed rendered or roughcast houses of character.	
28.	Nos. 68-72 Joy St.	A/B	Taller two-storey brick houses, with billets below the eaves, and a central coach-archway.	
	LITTLE MAY STREET:			
29.	No. 36, Little May St.	A	This house constitutes part of an important group with the terrace at Nos. 14-26 Joy Street.	
30.	Nos. 38-42, Little May Street.	A	Fine three-storey brick houses with console brackets to the hoods of the doorcases.	
31.	No. 44, Little May Street/ Nos. 13 and 15, Rathbone Street.	B	An old two-storey store with possibilities for conversion.	
	HAMILTON STREET:NORTH SIDE			
32.	The Citadel Pub, No. 1 Hamilton Street/No. 39 Cromac Square	A	A fine two-storey late Victorian stucco pub, with good detailing, quoins, cornice, and pilasters with festooned capitals.	
33.	No. 3 Hamilton Street	X	The ground-floor of the Abercorn town-house; now faceless in the contemporary commercial manner. See 'Buildings of Belfast', "The large and once-elegant house at 3 Hamilton Street (demolished 1962) was built in 1818 as a town residence of the Duke of Abercorn's family. It had an unusual doorway framed by Roman Ionic columns, and a stone lintel with stucco bunches of grapes attached."	Brett, p.20
34.	Nos. 7-19 Hamilton Street	A	A fine mixed bunch of three-storey houses, earlier than most in the district, some still residential, some used for commercial purposes. No. 7 has a large pointed doorcase, spoiled by a large placard. No. 19 has glazing bars and fanlight complete.	
35.	Blitzed site, formerly Nos. 21/23 Hamilton Street	X	Small car park, behind hoarding.	
36.	Nos. 25-29 Hamilton Street	X	Modern two-storey redbrick engineering workshop.	
37.	Nos. 31-33 Hamilton Street	X	Fiesta Ballroom (now vacant, and for sale) and paint store; modern, garish, and unsightly.	
38.	No. 35 Hamilton Street	B	A three-storey brick house without glazing bars, of no particular note.	
39.	No. 37 Hamilton Street	X	A grimly wrong-headed piece of modern redbrick infill.	
40.	Nos. 39 and 41 Hamilton Street	A	Good three-storey brick houses with quoins and glazing bars complete; No. 41 has a very nice honeysuckle-design fanlight.	

a

a St. Malachy's Church
b 20-26a, Hamilton Street
c 54, Joy Street
d For comparison: the false backs (to University Street) of
a terrace in Mount Charles; formerly dreary; recently well
repainted by the University to specifications suggested by
the Ulster Architectural Heritage Society

c

b

d

No.	Building	Class	Date, Type, Architect, etc.	References
	HAMILTON STREET:SOUTH SIDE			
41.	Nos. 10-14 Hamilton Street	B	Three storey stucco houses, with Regency glazing bars; small shops; No. 12, "The Marve".	
42.	Vacant Site, formerly Nos. 16-18 Hamilton Street	X	Surrounded by a high prison-camp fence, whether to keep the litter in or out is uncertain.	
43.	Nos. 20-30 Hamilton Street	A	A splendid Georgian three-storey stucco terrace, the best of its kind in Belfast. There is elaborate incised Greek-key pattern ornament in the pilasters, frieze, and in the pilasters and lintels of the doorcases; there are acroteria on the parapet at the heads of the main pilasters; No. 30 incorporates a coach-arch giving access to the yard (now builder's yard) at the rear. See 'Buildings of Belfast'. Very seedy and run-down, but well worth restoration.	Brett, p.20
44.	Nos. 32 and 34 Hamilton Street	A	Probably the earliest houses in the street - they project forward into the streetline. Small stuccoed three-storey houses with quoins, a few glazing-bars left; No. 32 has a nice rectangular fanlight.	
45.	Nos. 36-46 Hamilton Street with No. 11 Catherine Street North	A	Excellent three-storey redbrick terrace houses, with glazing-bars almost intact. Nos. 38 and 40 have delightful curly wrought-iron fanlights; all have arched doorcases with minuscule pilasters; quoins.	
	SUSSEX PLACE, NORTH SIDE:			
46.	Nos. 5 and 7 Sussex Place	X	Characterless commercial buildings.	
	SUSSEX PLACE, SOUTH SIDE:			
47.	No. 2 Sussex Place.	A	A pleasant four-bay house of painted brick, with glazing bars complete, incorporating Carson's newsagents shop, where the small girls from the Convent School opposite spend their pocket-money on sweeties, a penn'orth at a time.	
48.	Vacant site, formerly Nos. 6-18 Sussex Place	X	The bones of No. 4 remain to prop up its neighbour. This was an admirably dignified stucco terrace, with hooded doorcases; demolished 1970 to make way for a carpark and hoardings, thereby destroying the visual continuity of the link from Alfred Street to Cromac Street.	
	RUSSEL STREET, NORTH SIDE			
49.	Nos. 24-28, Russel Street	B	Two-storeyed brick houses, Nos. 24 and 26 painted, No. 28 with an attic.	
50.	Nos. 30 and 32 Russell Street	A/B	Gaily-painted tiny two-storey houses in the shadow of St. Malachy's; they might make one good house if well modernised.	
	RUSSELL STREET, SOUTH SIDE			
51.	Nos. 27-37 Russell Street	B	Cheerfully painted brick two-storey houses, Nos. 31 and 37 with pleasant rectangular fanlights.	

*U*lster
*A*rchitectural
*H*eritage
*S*ociety

30 College Gardens
Belfast, 9

The Society, formed in 1967, is non-profit-making, non-political, non-sectarian, and is recognised as a charity for tax purposes. While it is based in Belfast, its membership and interests extend throughout the nine counties of the province of Ulster. Its objects are: to promote the appreciation and enjoyment of good architecture of all periods; to encourage the preservation of buildings and groups of artistic merit or historic importance; and to encourage public awareness and appreciation of the beauty, history and character of local neighbourhoods.

The Society is engaged in the preparation and publication of a series of surveys and lists of buildings and groups of importance in Ulster. The following lists have already been published, or will be published shortly:

1.	Queen's University area of Belfast	8.	Antrim and Ballymena
2.	Lurgan and Portadown	9.	Downpatrick
3.	Moira R.D.C.	10.	City of Derry
4.	Lisburn	11.	Town of Monaghan
5.	Banbridge	12.	West Antrim
6.	Portaferry and Strangford	13.	Dungannon and Cookstown
7.	Craigavon Urban District	14.	Craigavon (omnibus edition)
		15.	Derry — Rural Areas

If you have found this list of interest, you may wish to order others, or to place a standing order for the Society's publications. Or you may wish to become a member: membership of the Society costs £1 a year; for those under 25, 50p · life membership, £20; corporate membership, £5 a year, or £25 for ten years.

Please cut along these lines

MEMBERSHIP FORM

I wish to become:
a full member ☐ £1 herewith
an under-25 member ☐ 50p herewith
a life member ☐ £20 herewith
for one year ending 31st December 19 . . ☐
completed banker's order herewith ☐
completed deed of covenant herewith ☐

(signature) . . . .

(address) . . . .

. . . .

To: Ulster Architectural Heritage Society,

30 College Gardens, Belfast, 9

BANKER'S ORDER

To (Banker) . . . .

. . . .

(Branch) . . . .

Please pay to the account of the Ulster Architectural Heritage Society, Belfast Banking Co. Ltd., Donegall Square North Branch, Belfast, the sum of £. . . . . my subscription until 31st December this year; and thereafter the sum of £. . . . . on each 1st January till further notice.

(signature). . . . .

(address). . . . .

. . . .

(date). . . . . .19. . . . .

Please cut along this line

The Society formed in 1967 is a non-profit-making, non-political organisation and is recognised as such for tax purposes. While based in Belfast, its membership and interests extend throughout the nine counties of the province of Ulster. Its objects are: to promote the appreciation and enjoyment of good architecture of all periods; to encourage the preservation of buildings and groups of particular merit or historic importance; and to encourage public awareness and appreciation of the beauty, history and character of local neighbourhoods.

The Society is engaged in the preparation and publication of a series of surveys and lists of buildings and groups of importance in Ulster. The following lists have already been published or will be published shortly:

1. Queen's University area or Belfast
2. Lurgan and Portadown
3. Moira R.D.C.
4. Lisburn
5. Banbridge
6. Portaferry and Strangford
7. Craigavon Urban District

8. Antrim and Ballymena
9. Downpatrick
10. City of Derry
11. Town of Monaghan
12. West Antrim
13. Dungannon and Cookstown
14. Craigavon (rural edition)
15. Derry – Rural Area

If you have found this list of interest, you may wish to order others, or to place a standing order for the Society's publications. Or you may wish to become a member. Membership of the Society costs £1 a year (for those under 25, 50p), life membership £20; corporate membership, £5 a year, or £25 for ten years.

MEMBERSHIP FORM

BANKER'S ORDER

To: Ulster Architectural Heritage Society,
30 College Gardens, Belfast, 9